A long time ago, as a li
I dreamed of traveling all ov

... And often I'd ask about the past
Driving everyone crazy fast!

Little Miss HISTORY Travels to
ELLIS ISLAND
© 2015 Barbara Ann Mojica. All Rights Reserved.

Published in The UNITED STATES of AMERICA
eugenus® STUDIOS, LLC
P.O. BOX 112
CRARYVILLE, NY 12521
E-Mail: Barbara@LittleMissHistory.com
WebSite: www.LittleMissHISTORY.com

ISBN-13: 978-0988503069
ISBN-10: 0988503069

In Loving Memory of My Grandma

Elizabeth Fertig

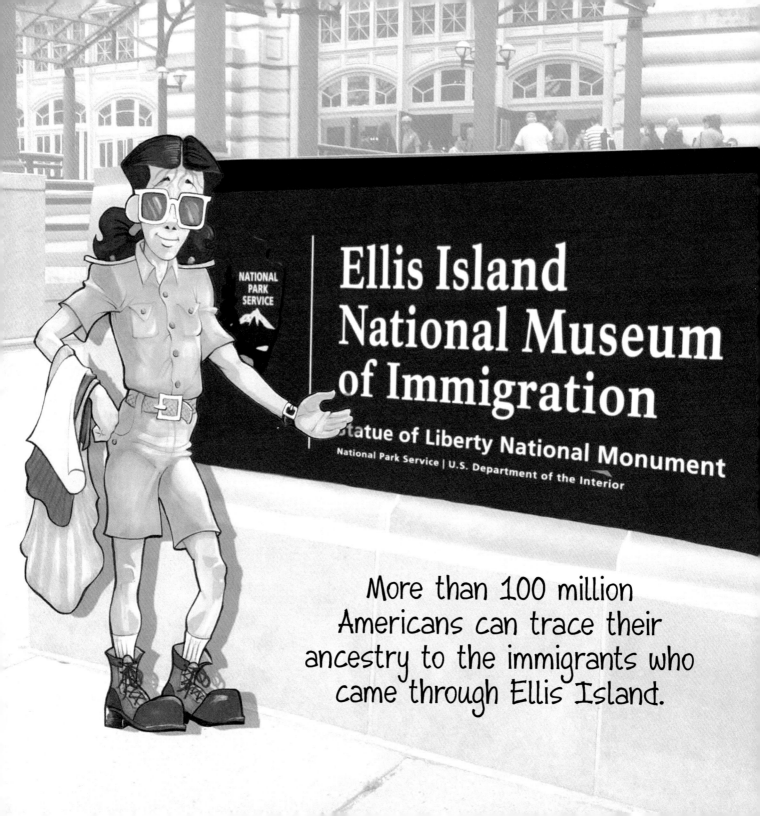

More than 100 million Americans can trace their ancestry to the immigrants who came through Ellis Island.

Before Ellis Island opened in 1892, immigrants passed through Castle Garden Immigration Center across the bay in Manhattan.

Ellis Island began its life as a three acre sand bar. Samuel Ellis, a butcher, agreed to sell it to New York State. In 1808 the state transferred it to the federal government to serve as a military base, Fort Gibson. After the War of 1812, they abandoned the fort and used it to store weapons.

The Federal Bureau of Immigration renamed it Ellis Island in 1891.

The original wooden building on
Ellis Island burned after five years.

The new main building opened in 1900. William Alciphron Boring and Edward Lippincott Tilton received gold medals for its design.

Annie Moore, a fifteen year old Irish immigrant, disembarked first. She got an official greeting ...

... and a $10 gold coin. That was the most money that she had ever owned.

From 1894 to 1924, more than 70 per cent of all immigrants came through the port of New York.

... while the poorer immigrants had to walk single file through the Great Hall to face inspection.

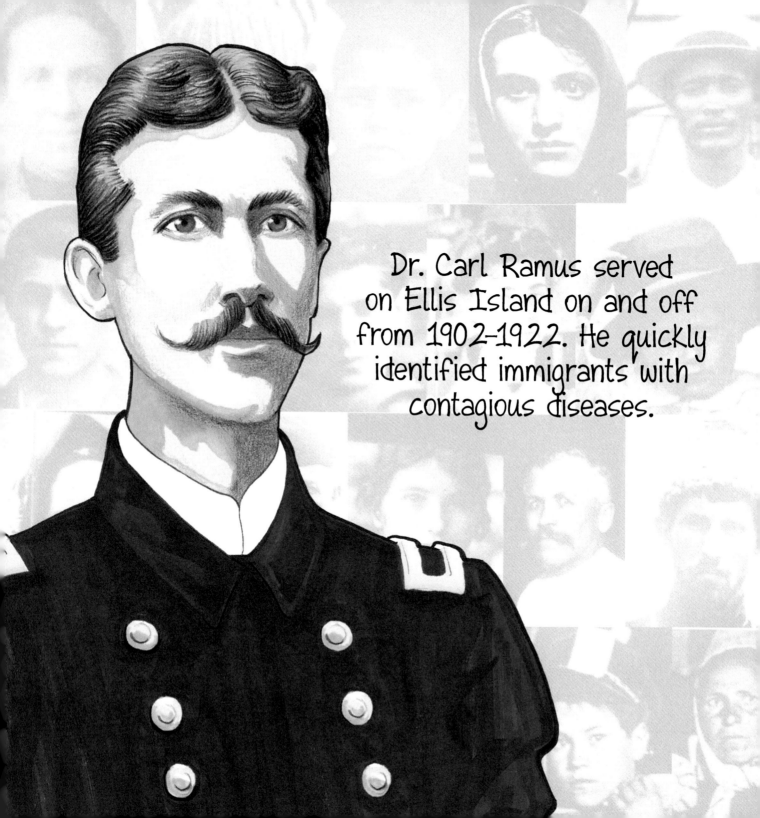

Dr. Carl Ramus served on Ellis Island on and off from 1902-1922. He quickly identified immigrants with contagious diseases.

Medical examiners closely observed the immigrants as they climbed the staircase.

Harvey E. Snider worked here as a gatekeeper, watchman, guard, and clerk. He rose to Chief Inspector supervising the entire night staff on Ellis Island.

About 2% of all immigrants were sent back home because of disease, insanity or criminal background.

Augustus F. Sherman photographed detained immigrants in native costume. As Chief Clerk he heard the appeals from rejected immigrants. He decided who could enter the country.

Those who failed inspection were sent home or placed in the hospital on the island.

More than three thousand died while waiting.

Ellis Island received the nicknames,
"The Island of Tears" or "Heartbreak Island."

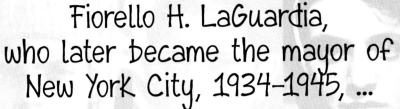

Fiorello H. LaGuardia,
who later became the mayor of
New York City, 1934–1945, ...

... translated German,
Italian, Yiddish
and Croatian for
immigrants on
Ellis Island.

Immigrants who passed inspection had to answer 29 questions.

1. Number on (passenger) list.
2. Name in Full.
3. Age
4. Sex
5. Married / Single
6. Occupation
7. Able to Read / Write
8. Nationality, Country/ City/Town
9. Race
10. Last Residence
11. Name & Address of relative in native country
12. Final Destination
13. No. on list
14. Whether having a ticket to final destination.
15. By whom was passage paid?
16. Whether in possession of $50.
17. Whether ever in U.S. before.
8. Whether going to join relative if so, list name and address.
19. Ever in prison, almshouse institution for care of insane etc.
20. Whether a Polygamistt.
21. Whether an Anarchist.
22. Whether coming with an offer promise, or agreement of labor.
23. Condition of Health
24. Deformed or crippled
25. Height
26. Complexion
27. Color of eyes/hair
28. Identifying marks
29. Place of Birth

Immigrants who passed inspection met relatives and friends outside the Registry Room by ...

During World War II, Ellis Island served as a prison for German merchant sailors and others suspected of spying or sabotage.

After 1950, the U.S. Government passed strict laws controlling immigration of those suspected ...

... to have Communist sympathies. They set up quotas that cut down the number of immigrants allowed entry.

The whole south side
of Ellis Island is
called the "sad side"
and is now off limits.

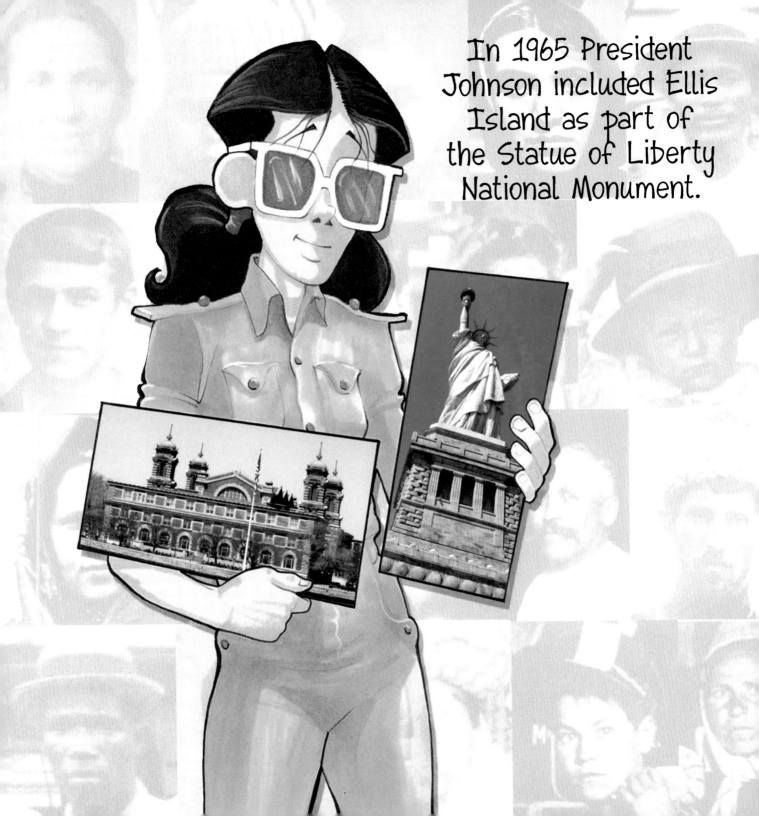

In 1965 President Johnson included Ellis Island as part of the Statue of Liberty National Monument.

Lyndon B. Johnson
36th President of
the United States

The main building
reopened in 1990
as a museum.

Where They Came From

From the early colonial period through the 19th century, the people who migrated to North America came primarily from northern and western Europe. During the 18th century, enslaved Africans arrived in large numbers as well. By the mid-19th century, immigrants began arriving from new regions of the world, especially Asia and southern and eastern Europe.

This map shows the major regions of origin of those who came to North America between 1620 and 1890.

Map labels (Where They Came From)

NORWAY · SWEDEN · JAPAN · RUSSIA · NETHERLANDS · GERMAN LANDS · DENMARK · POLAND · BOHEMIA · SCOTLAND · IRELAND · HUNGARY · CHINA · PACIFIC OCEAN · ENGLAND · BELGIUM · ITALY · GREECE · FRANCE · NORTH AMERICA · PORTUGAL · SPAIN · SWITZERLAND · SENEGAMBIA · ATLANTIC OCEAN · SIERRA LEONE · KONGO · IVORY COAST · ANGOLA · GOLD COAST · BIGHT OF BENIN · SOUTH AMERICA

Legend: 1620s – 1690 · until 1808 · 1850s – 1870s · 1850s – 1890

Map years (right side)

1783 · 1810 · 1854 · 1890

1680

- BRITISH
- FRENCH
- SPANISH

Als

States came at the expense

... 9th century, they

HELD BY NATIVE AMERICANS

... BY NATIVE AMERICANS

Farmers, Artisans, and Utopians

German speakers, three million strong, made up the largest immigrant group in U.S. history through the end of the 19th century — a diverse community with a strong ethnic identity.

In 1998, The United States Supreme Court settled a boundary dispute between New York and New Jersey.

They declared that most of the island is in New Jersey.

Today the
National Park Service
operates Ellis Island.

The United States
Park Police, Marine Patrol
guard the waterways.

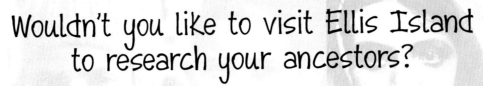

Wouldn't you like to visit Ellis Island to research your ancestors?

You can do so at stations like this.

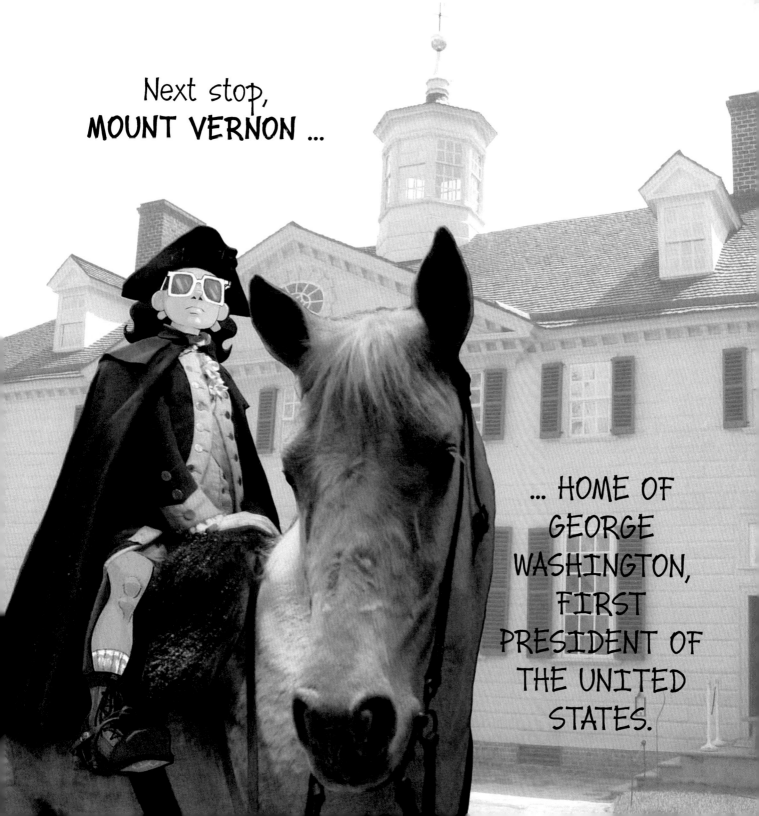

Made in the USA
Middletown, DE
27 September 2016